LEARN HOW TO PLAY THE U

T0085643

ASAP

UKULELE

A NEW EASY SELF-TEACHING METHOD

BY RON MIDDLEBROOK

ISBN 978-1-57424-258-4
SAN 683-8022

Special thanks to Louis Wu of Ohana Ukuleles for the cover photo of the Ohana SK-350G ukulele.

The web site of the fine "Ohana Ukuleles" is: www.ohanaukuleles.com

Thanks to Mark Lewis for taking the Ohana photos.

Thanks to Robert Armstrong for permission to use "Beachless Bob's Strums for the Ukulele" and the "King Bennie Nawahi" story.

Cover by James Creative Group

Copyright © 2010 CENTERSTREAM Publishing, LLC
P.O. Box 17878 - Anaheim Hills, CA 92817

www.centerstream-usa.com

All rights for publication and distribution are reserved.
No part of this book may be reproduced in any form or by any Electronic or mechanical means including information storage and retrieval systems
without permission in writing from the publisher, except by reviewers who may quote brief passages in review.

CONTENTS

ANCIENT GODS OF HAWAII

The gods of ancient Hawaii still hold sway over portions of the Islands. For instance, many modern gardens have the ferocious Tiki gods standing guard at the gate much as they used to guard the sacred heiau (temple). The ruins of countless heiaus with the mystery of their ancient worship are still found today on all the islands. Many rocks and shapeless stones are looked on with awe for the spirit of the god they are said to represent.

Four primal gods and hundreds of lesser gods ruled the lives of ancient Polynesians. The principal gods were: Kane, the father-mother of man and all living things. He was the god of sunlight, water, nature and forests. Lono, the god of peace, agriculture, farming, rain …and therefore offerings were made to him of pigs, taro and sweet potatoes. Ku was the god of war and power, and this was the god to whom human sacrifices were made. Kanaloa was the god of the sea, and according to some authorities, also the "fallen angel" god who ruled the region of departed spirits.

There are hundreds of minor deities, too. The canoe makers had one god, the bird-catchers another. Those who fished or sailed canoes worshipped still other gods. To be sure of good fishing, fishermen left offerings of sacred rocks and food to the fish gods.

Almost any material object, such as an image, a bird, a fish or a mere shapeless stone, might represent a god. These carved images or animals or other objects were not supposed to be the god himself – they were symbols of the god, or they were a repository for the mana (spirit) of the god.

Among the animals thus representing gods were the owl (pueo) who was a helpful god, and the lizard (mo'o) who was most wicked. The rat, mud hen, goose, various fishes were other god spirits, and even the ti plant was felt to be so sacred that placing ti leaves about the house was purported to ward off evil spirits. Hula girls dance in ti leaf skirts today, and dancing was first a sacred manner of telling a story.

Each of the major gods had his own temple. Modern visitors can explore the remains of many of these heiaus. Outside every heiau were idols or images carved of wood. Today, these images with the monstrous mouths are carved from tree fern, and called tiki gods – which is really a Tahitian name – and are considered good luck. So they are used in gardens and hotels as part of the Polynesian décor. The grimacing faces and general ugliness of the image were a symbol of power and ferocity – and a gesture of defiance to any lesser power.

The images were sometimes carried by the high kahuna (priest) to inspire awe in him and the people. Each chief had his particular image of the war-god that was carried into battle with him. At harvest time, when taxes in the form of produce were brought to the chiefs, a wooden god stood guard over the transaction.

It was Queen Kaahumanu who began breaking the old kapus (forbidden things) connected with the old religion. And Hewahewa, the high priest, set fire to some of the idols and the heiaus.

This was the beginning of the collapse of the ancient worship – but many ruins remain today to remind one of the old ways.

Parts of the Ukelele

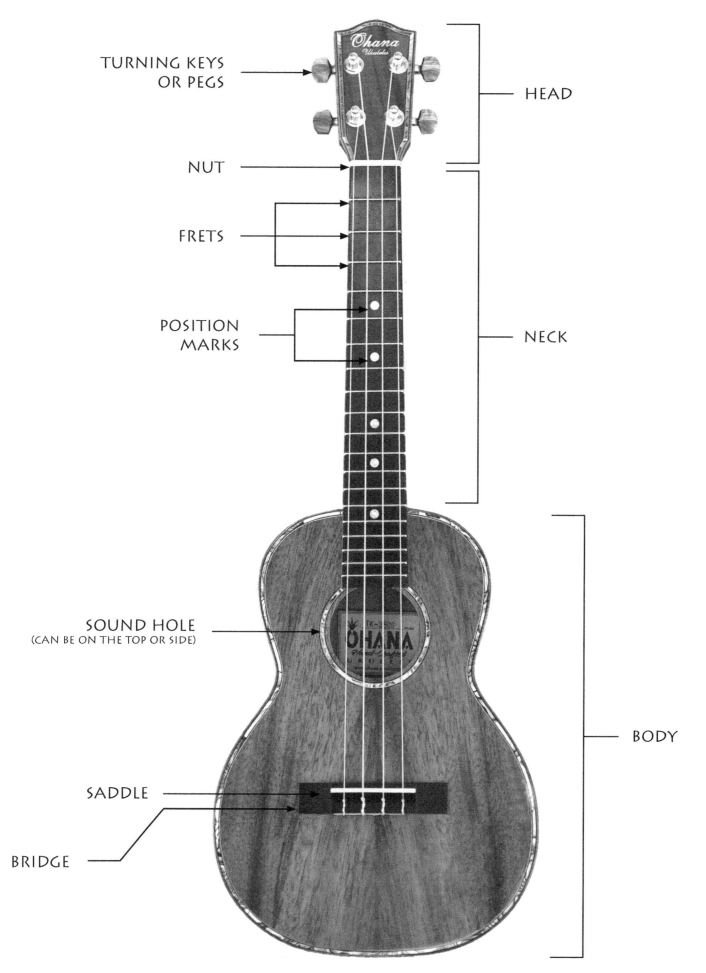

TURNING KEYS
OR PEGS

HEAD

NUT

FRETS

POSITION
MARKS

NECK

SOUND HOLE
(CAN BE ON THE TOP OR SIDE)

SADDLE

BRIDGE

BODY

Types Of Ukuleles

Soprano

The Soprano ukulele is usually the smallest size and normally tuned to "GCEA", "A" being the first string (4321). It's the typical Hawaiian tuning and is the characteristic sound of the Ukulele. The "G" or 4th string is pitched higher then the "C" or 1st string. The old familiar "My Dog Has Fleas" tuning. The small size makes it a favorite for many and especially for young players.

Concert

Slightly larger and for many, the perfect size since it has a larger fretboard better suited for those with larger hands. The tone and sound reflects the slightly deeper body giving it a little deeper, mellow sound. The tuning is the same, GCEA.

Tenor

Still larger then the Concert in body and fretboard, this give it a much deeper sound. Especially appreciated by advanced musicians. The tuning is the same, GCEA.

The Banjo Ukulele

You can't miss it. A short neck with a round banjo head. Tuned the same, GCEA, and the size is pretty much the size of the Concert or Tenor. Louder in sound then the others. A favorite instrument of the roaring 20's.

Baritone

The big daddy of the Ukulele family sometimes called the little guitar since the tuning is the same as the first 4 strings of the guitar, DGBE (low to high 4321). For guitar players the Baritone ukulele is a great companion to the other sizes of ukulele.

Soprano   Concert   Tenor   Baritone

How to tune your Ukulele, G C E A (C Tuning)

Pitch Pipe.

1. Tune the 1st String (A) until it sounds exactly the same as A on the Pitch Pipe.
2. Tune the 2nd string (E) until it sounds exactly the same as E on the Pitch Pipe.
3. Tune the 3rd string (C) and the 4th string (G) in the same manor.

Relative Tuning

Whenever a pitch pipe or another tuned instrument is not available for tuning, the "relative tuning" method can be used. The Uke will be in tune with itself, but not necessarily in tune with any other instrument.

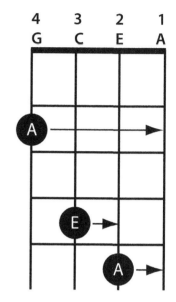

1. Tighten the 1st string (A) until it is fairly tight and produces a high tone.
2. Press the 5th fret of the 2nd string (E) and tune to equal the pitch of the 1st string (A). Photo #2
3. Press the 4th fret of the 3rd string (C) and tune to equal the pitch of the 2nd string (E). Photo #3
4. Press the 2nd fret of the 4th string (G) and tune to equal the pitch of the 1st string (A). Photo #4
5. Go slow, if you feel like you have tuned past the pitch, lower the string and start over.

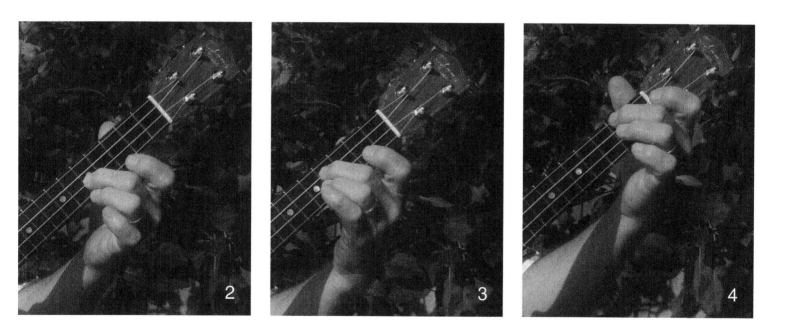

How to Begin

Correct Playing Position

The middle of the right forearm should press the back of the ukulele to the body, firmly enough to prevent its slipping so it may be played in either a sitting or standing position.

With the handy Centerstream ukulele strap, using the strap takes the pressure off the fretting hand.

The left arm should be extended forward. Holding the neck of the ukulele between the thumb and joint of the first finger, with the tip of the thumb resting approximately at the side of the first fret.

Position of the Left or Fretting Hand and Fingers

Study these pictures carefully; notice the position of the thumb, resting at the side of the neck near the first fret. The finger is curved in position to contact the strings, and the palm is held away from the neck.

The front view shows the fingers in place for chording. Notice that only the fingertips are used and placed behind the frets not on them.

The back view shows the position of the thumb.

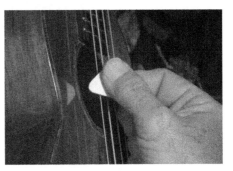

Using the Pick
The pick can be felt which will give a softer sound or any of the picks that are on the market today. Hold the pick lightly but firmly between your thumb and first finger and strum up and down the strings just above the sound hole. Keep the wrist relaxed.

The Common Stroke

There are several different strokes that are effective in various styles of music. For the present we give only the "Common" stroke that is the basis of all the others and must be thoroughly mastered before any of the more complicated strums are attempted. The Common Stroke is made by dragging the first finger of the right hand lightly down and up across all the strings at the upper edge of the sound hole.

Try to relax the hand at all times, the stroke being made entirely with the wrist which must be perfectly free in its motion. Keep the wrist high. Make the down stroke squarely on the nail of the first finger, and the up stroke with the ball of fleshy part. Don't forget to study "Beachless Bob's Strums for the Ukulele' throughtout this book for more crowd pleasing strums

TABLATURE

All of the music in this book will be written in standard music notation (on top) and tablature (on bottom). In Tablature there are 4 lines, each representing a string on the ukulele. Numbers are placed in the lines corresponding to the frets on which you place your fingers. The "O" means it's an open string.

HERE IS AN EXAMPLE OF THE MUSIC WITH THE TABLATURE

Annie Laurie

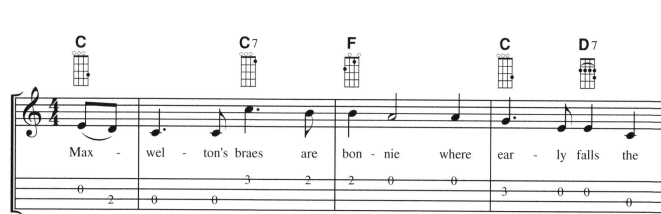

NOTES ON THE UKULELE FINGERBOARD

The example shows the notes on the fingerboard up to the 12th fret (one octave). If you see a sharp symbol (♯) by the note it means to "raise" the pitch one fret higher. The flat symbol (♭) means to "lower" the pitch one fret back.

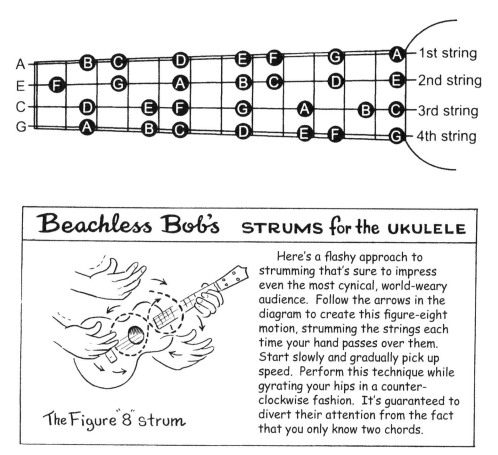

Beachless Bob's STRUMS for the UKULELE

Here's a flashy approach to strumming that's sure to impress even the most cynical, world-weary audience. Follow the arrows in the diagram to create this figure-eight motion, strumming the strings each time your hand passes over them. Start slowly and gradually pick up speed. Perform this technique while gyrating your hips in a counter-clockwise fashion. It's guaranteed to divert their attention from the fact that you only know two chords.

The Figure "8" strum

Beachless Bob's STRUMS for the UKULELE

As soon as you've mastered the Figure 8 strum, try this show-stopping technique that's twice as effective. Follow the arrows in the diagram and with lots of practice and a little math you can double your skill level. As a challenge for you advanced players, alter your strumming pattern by multiples of eight for each successive chorus while performing your favorite tune.

The Figure "16" Strum

Beachless Bob's STRUMS for the UKULELE

Double Thumbing

This technique was borrowed from an age-old method of playing the five-string banjo known as "frailing". In some parts of North Carolina it's called "frooling" and in one particular county of Tennessee, the locals refer to the technique as "freeking the banjo". A diary entry by Thomas Jefferson refers to slaves on his plantation, performing on their banjars with a multiple thumb method of strumming. When practicing this motion make sure that your thumbs alternate between the fourth and second strings with each downward strum.

Beachless Bob's STRUMS for the UKULELE

Here's a method that utilizes the same finger-flicking motion commonly used to launch a nasal nugget after a period of nostril mining. The index finger is "triggered" with the aid of the thumb to create a brisk attack of the strings. The other fingers follow the index finger downward then sweep the strings on the upward strum to repeat the pattern.

The Booger Flick

EXERCISE NO. 1 – CHORD COMBINATIONS – KEY OF C

C is a good beginning key: The three basic chords C, F, and G7 (see diagrams below) are easy to learn, and will enable you to accompany a good many familiar songs. Practice these chords until you can change positions quickly and easily. Then go on to the next group.

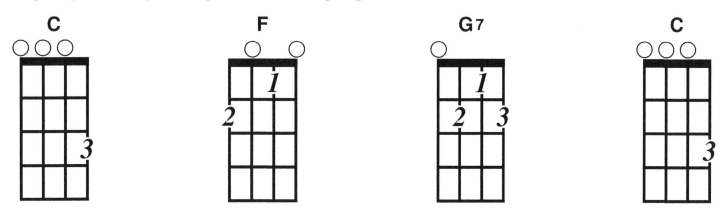

Two new chords were added: C7 and F minor. Practice this sequence in order, reading from left to right C, C7, F, Fmi and returning to C to finish.

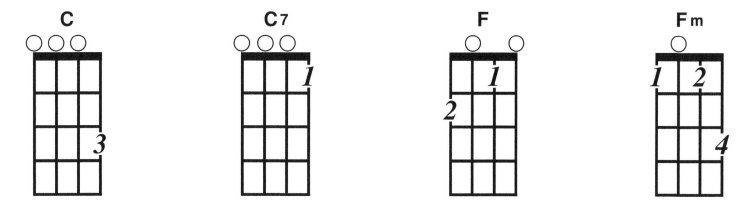

This next group of chords contains a pair of minor chords – Ami and Dmi frequently used in the key of C. Also E7 – one of the best and busiest chords on the uke. Practice these in sequence, too.

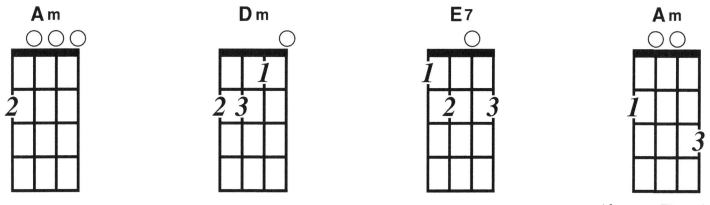

Alternate Fingering

Practice all of these chords until you know what each one sounds, feels and looks like! Then try out these two chord sequences and discover what a great combination they make:

1. C, C7, F, Fmi. C, G7, and C
2. C, E7, Ami, Dmi, E7 and Ami

After you've mastered these two combinations, try working out some of your own. *In some of the following songs I've sneaked in one or two different chords to learn, be on the lookout for them.*

My Bonnie Lies Over The Ocean

This arrangement copyright by Centerstream Publishing llc

Annie Laurie

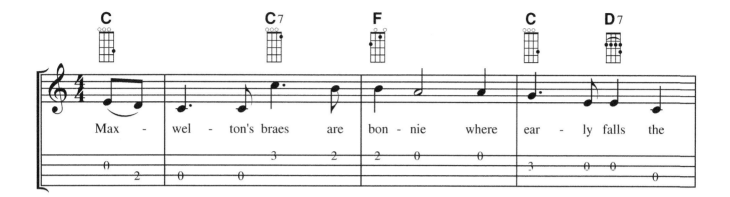

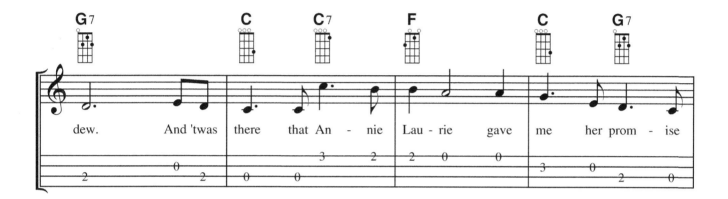

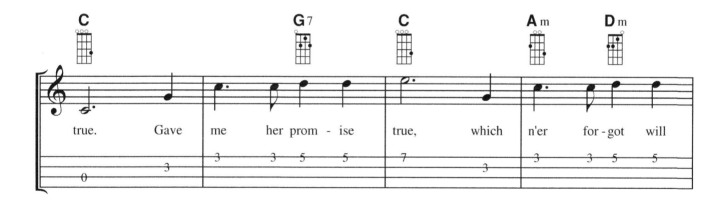

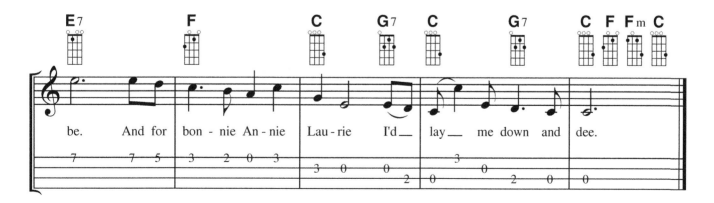

This arrangement copyright by Centerstream Publishing llc

On My Ukulele
(Tra La La La La)

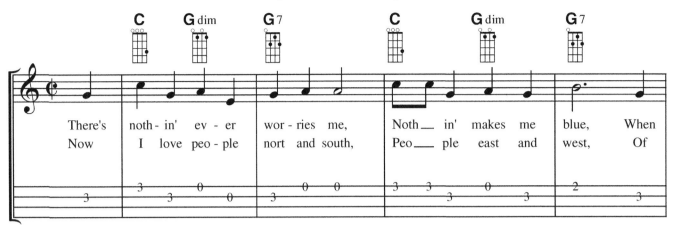

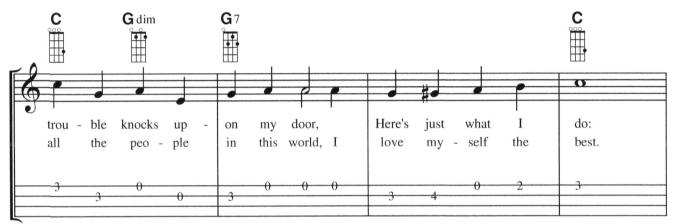

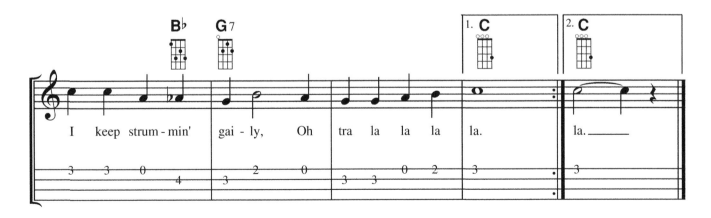

This arrangement copyright by Centerstream Publishing llc

Peg Of My Heart

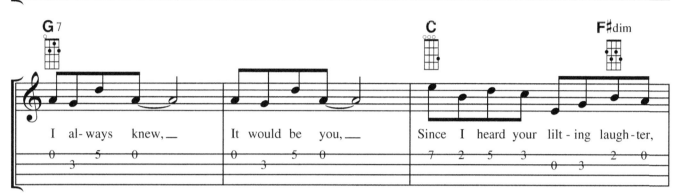

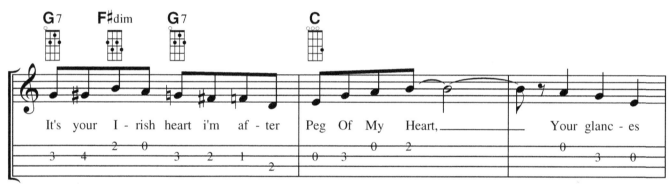

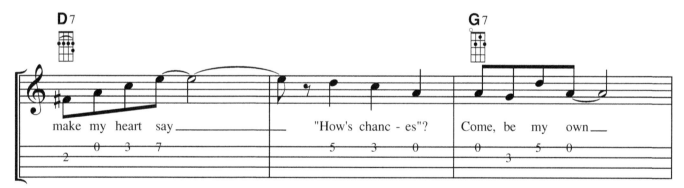

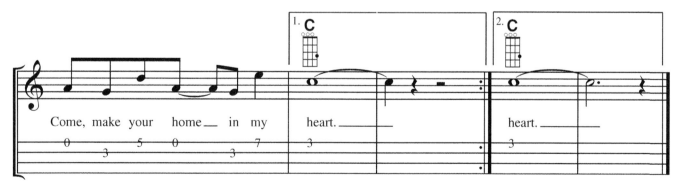

This arrangement copyright by Centerstream Publishing llc

When You Wore A Tulip
(And I Wore A Big Red Rose)

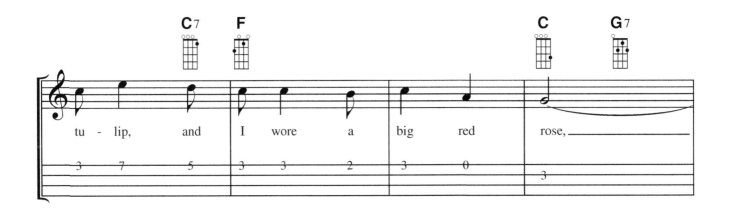

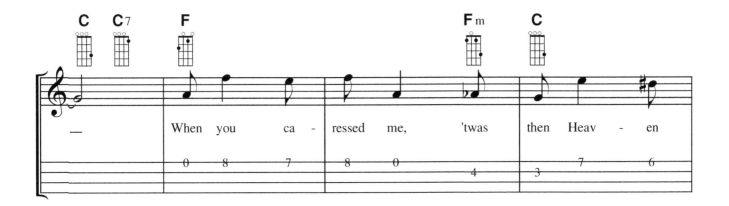

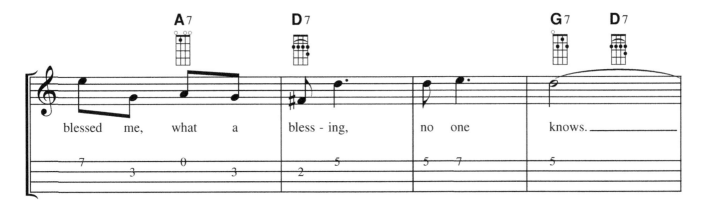

This arrangement copyright by Centerstream Publishing llc

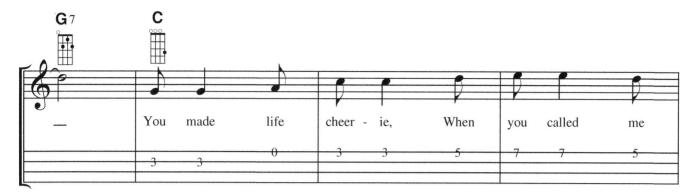

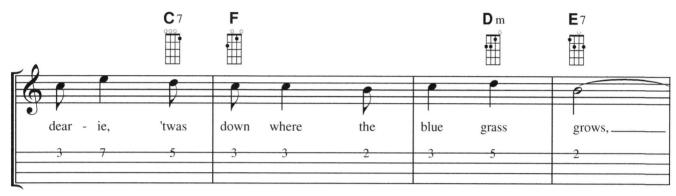

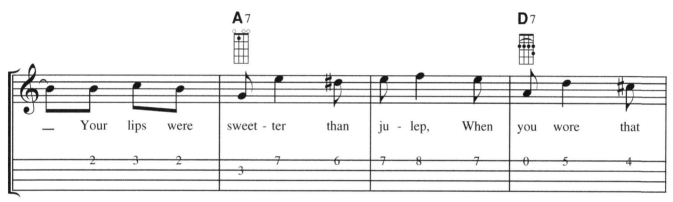

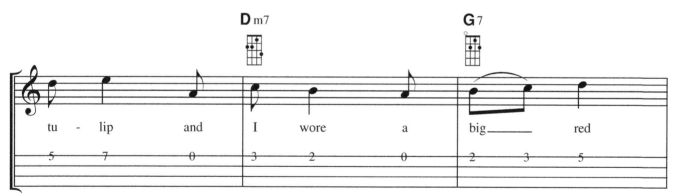

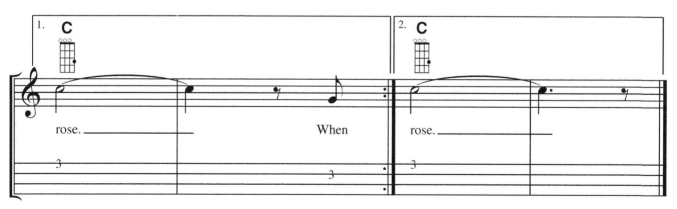

17

Exercise No. 2 – Chord Combinations – Key of F

F is a logical "next step" in these exercises – and a very useful key.

Again, let's start with the basic chords – F, B♭, C7, back to F.

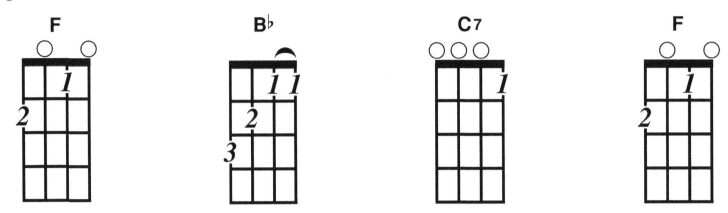

As with the first exercise in the key of C, practice these basic chords in order shown until you can change positions easily and naturally. Then on to the group below.

You'll find the F7 and D7 chords, very useful; also the B♭ minor. For a pretty chord sequence, try playing this combination: F, F7, B♭, B♭mi, F, C7, F.

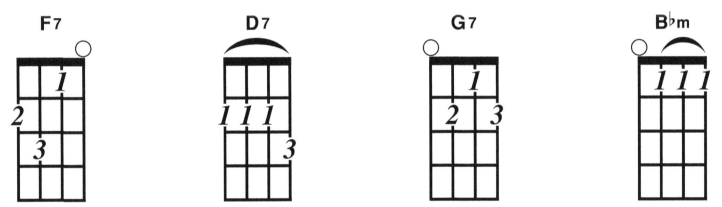

In the group below, Gmi and A7 will be new to you. Practice the chord sequence from left to right as shown below.

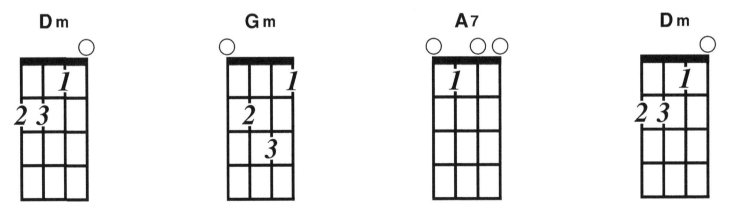

As you did with Exercise No. 1 – practice all these chords, individually and in the combinations indicated, until you get the "feel" of them and can play them easily and cleanly.

Once you've learned the chords in *just the two keys of C and F*, you'll discover that there are literally *dozens* of familiar songs you can accompany yourself on.

18

Auld Lang Syne

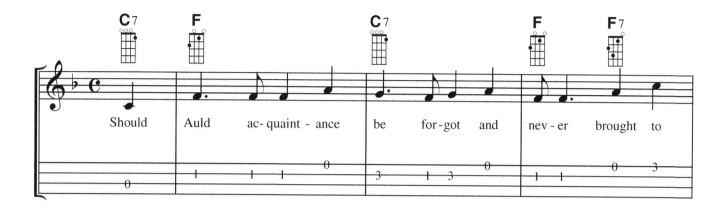

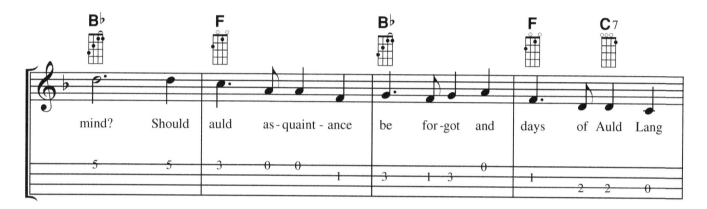

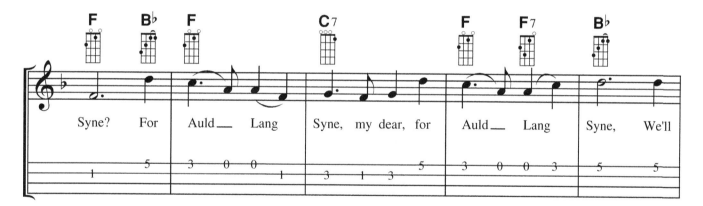

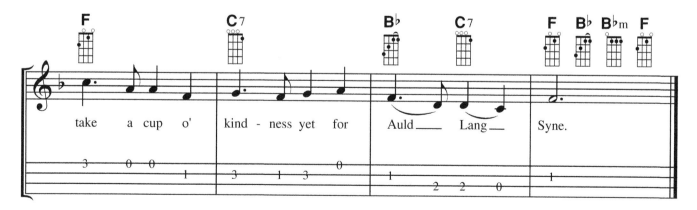

This arrangement copyright by Centerstream Publishing llc

Ukulele Lady

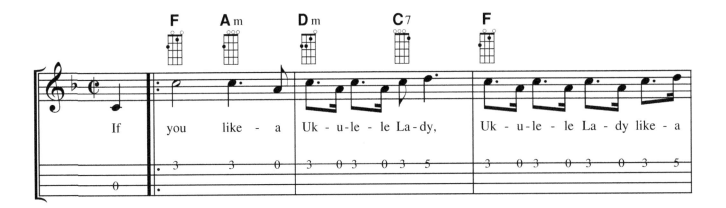

If you like - a Uk - u-le - le La - dy, Uk - u-le - le La - dy like - a

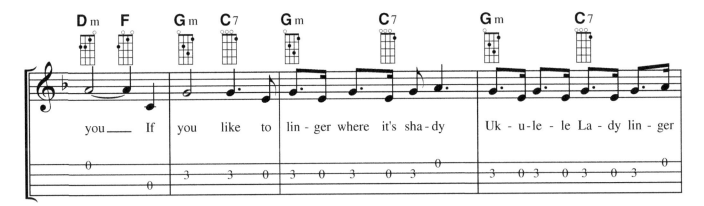

you___ If you like to lin - ger where it's sha - dy Uk - u-le - le La - dy lin - ger

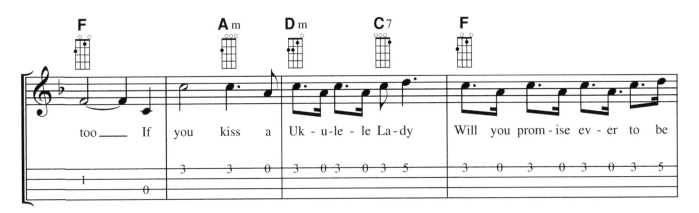

too___ If you kiss a Uk - u-le - le La - dy Will you prom - ise ev - er to be

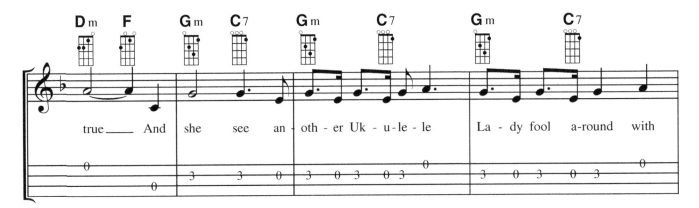

true___ And she see an - oth - er Uk - u-le - le La - dy fool a-round with

This arrangement copyright by Centerstream Publishing llc

She'll Be Comin' 'Round The Mountain

This arrangement copyright by Centerstream Publishing llc

Ja-Da

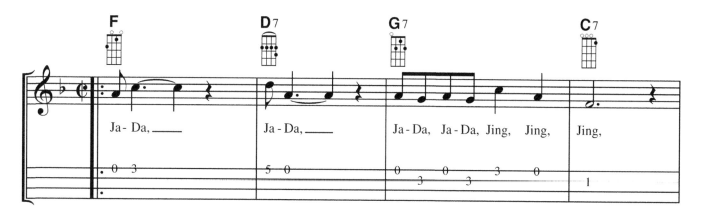

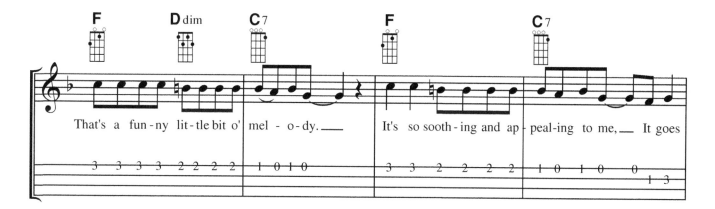

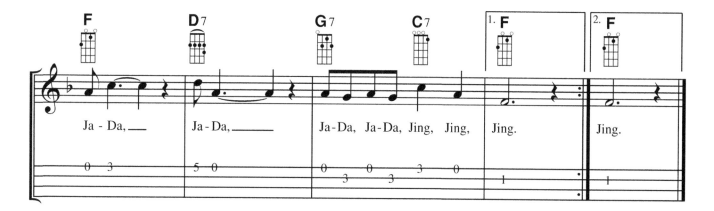

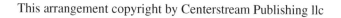

This arrangement copyright by Centerstream Publishing llc

I'm Always Chasing Rainbows

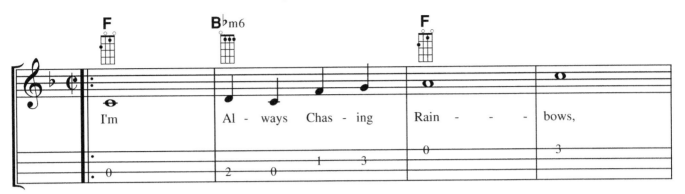

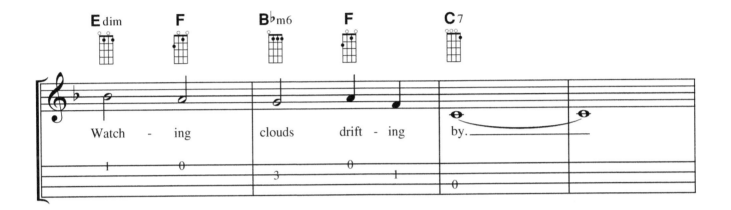

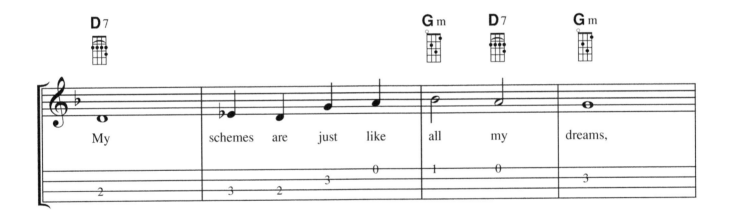

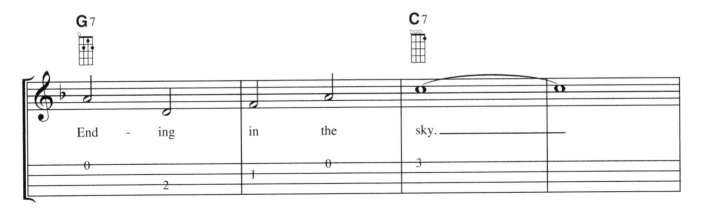

This arrangement copyright by Centerstream Publishing llc

24

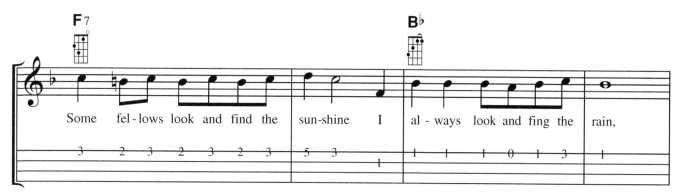

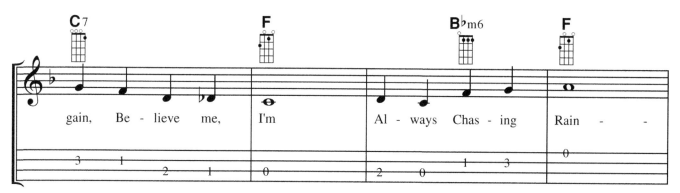

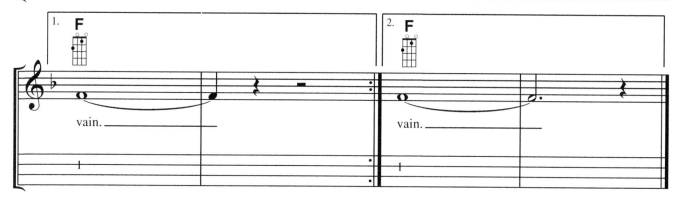

Exercise No. 3 – Chord Combinations – Key of G

As in the two previous exercises, we start out with the three basic chords – the "work horse" chords – in this key: G, C, D7 and back to G.

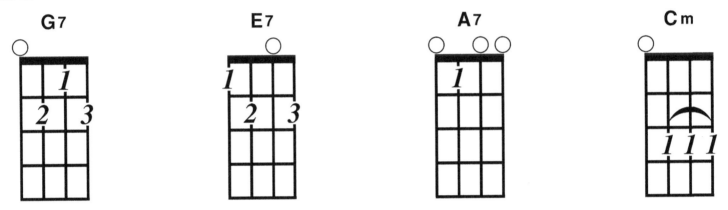

The only chord new to you in the group below is C minor.
Try playing G7, E7, A7, Cmi and back to G. Now, for variety, plays this combination: G, G7, C, Cmi, G, D7, and G.

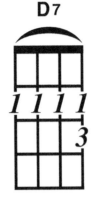

In the group below, two new chords have been added – Emi and B7. Practice them in connection with your old friend A minor. Play in order from left to right across the page as in previous exercises.

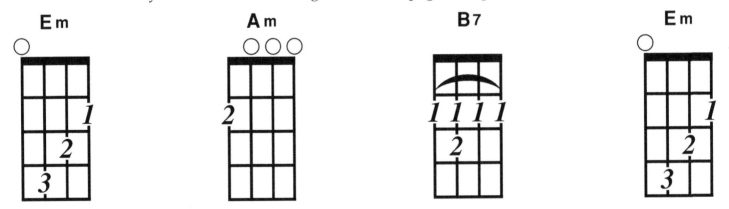

As a good chord-and-finger exercise, try the following chord combinations:
G, B7, A7, D7, and back to the G position. The only really tricky chord in this entire exercise is B7 – but with a little practice you'll soon have it eating out of your hand!
Go back and review exercises 1 and 2 and notice how many chords you learned there have carried over into this exercise. (Be on the look out for some surprise new chords in some of the following songs).

Now let's go to B♭ – in the next exercise!

Old Folks At Home

This arrangement copyright by Centerstream Publishing llc

27

Red River Valley

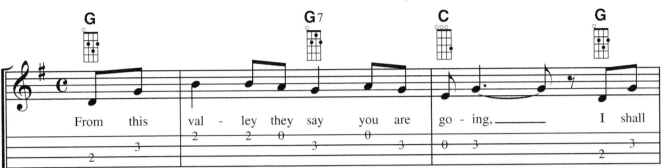

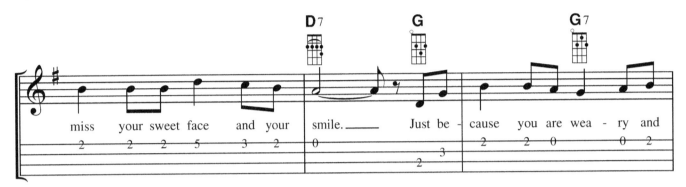

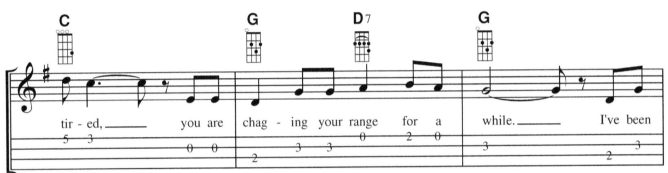

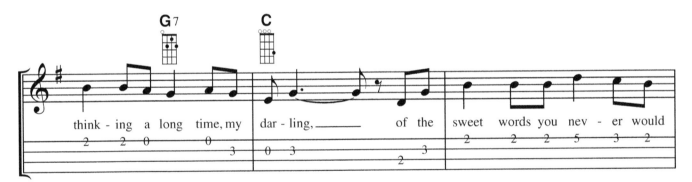

This arrangement copyright by Centerstream Publishing llc

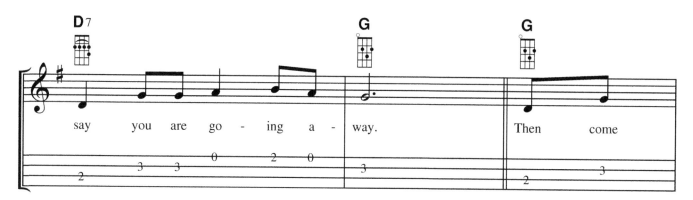

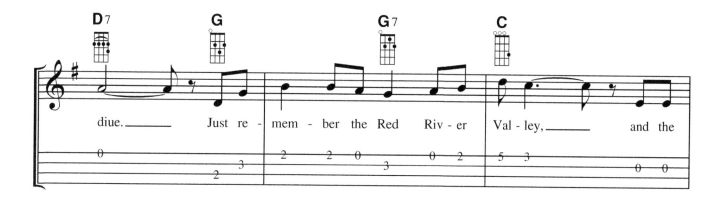

Red Wing

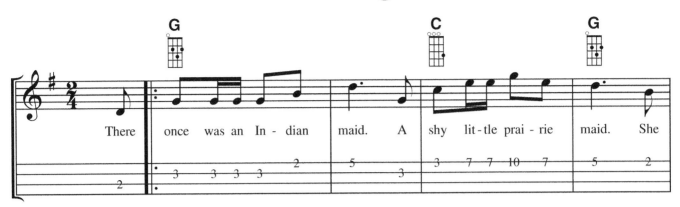

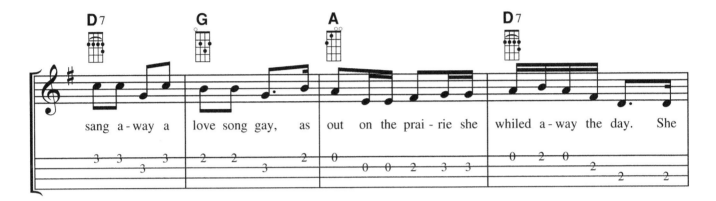

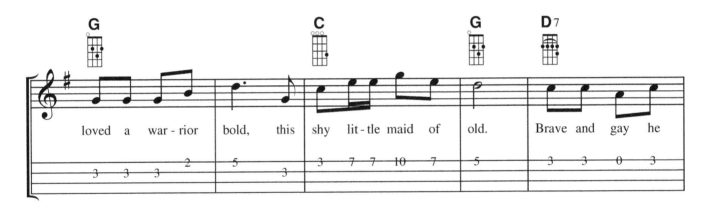

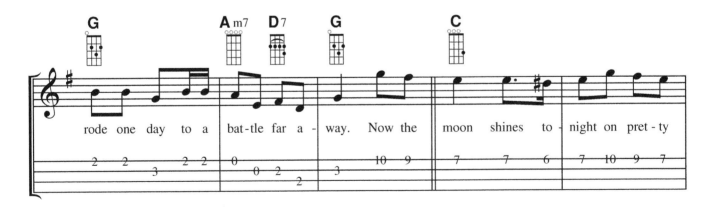

This arrangement copyright by Centerstream Publishing llc

Red Wing

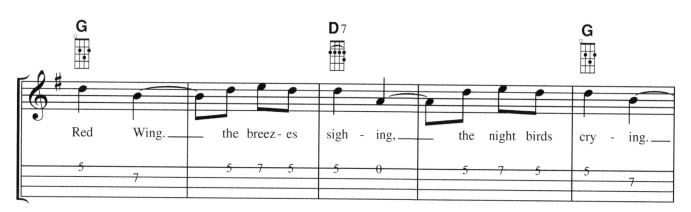

Red Wing.___ the breez-es sigh-ing,___ the night birds cry - ing.___

— So___ far be - neath the stars her brave is sleep - ing___

— while Red Wing's weep - ing___ her heart a - way. There way.

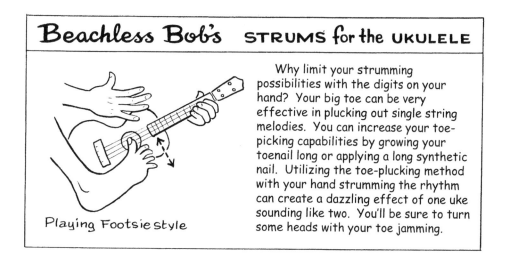

Beachless Bob's STRUMS for the UKULELE

Playing Footsie style

Why limit your strumming possibilities with the digits on your hand? Your big toe can be very effective in plucking out single string melodies. You can increase your toe-picking capabilities by growing your toenail long or applying a long synthetic nail. Utilizing the toe-plucking method with your hand strumming the rhythm can create a dazzling effect of one uke sounding like two. You'll be sure to turn some heads with your toe jamming.

Give Me A Ukulele
(And A Ukulele Baby)

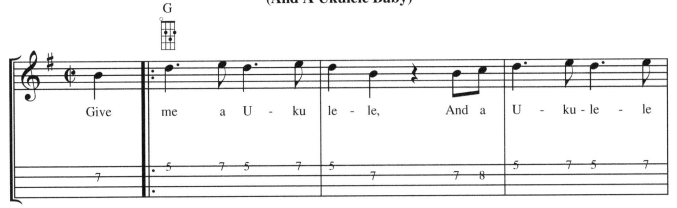

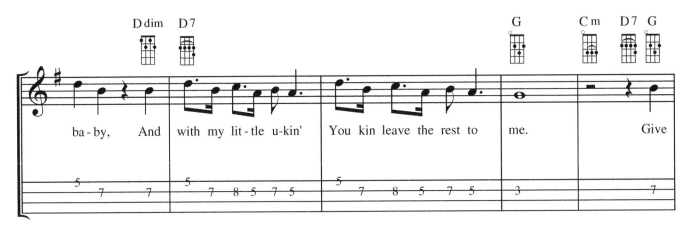

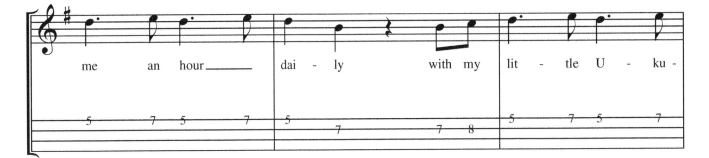

This arrangement copyright by Centerstream Publishing llc

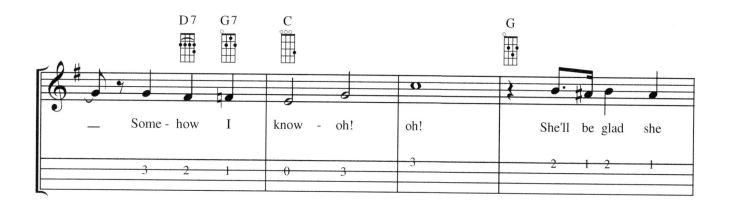

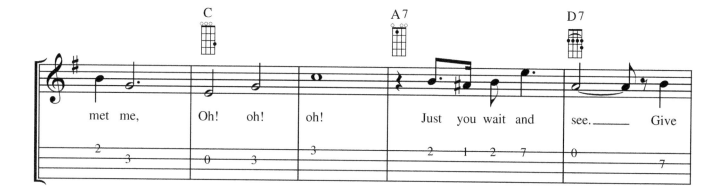

EXERCISE NO. 4 – CHORD COMBINATIONS – KEY OF B♭

Once more, let's begin by learning the three basic chords in B♭. They are :
B♭ (surprise!) E♭, F7. Play in the order shown.

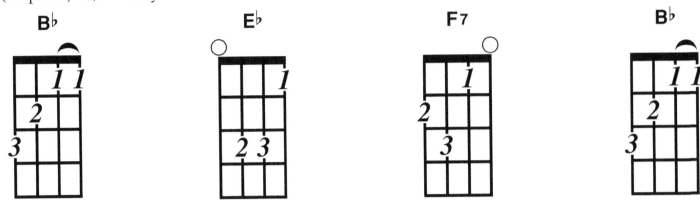

In the chords below something really new has been added: A second position for the E♭ and F7 chords. Practice them carefully. Try changing from E♭ to E♭ (2nd position) and from F7 to F7 (2nd position).

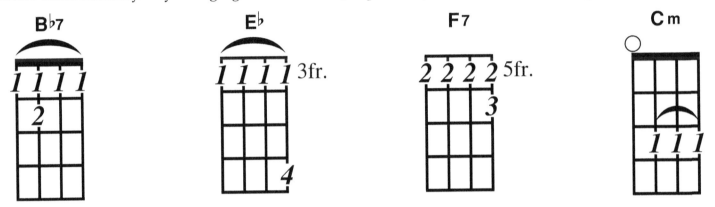

B♭ minor is the only new chord in the group below. You'll find the fingering a bit tricky at first, but practice it until your 3rd and 4th fingers go where they should! Try playing B♭, B♭7, E♭, E♭ mi, B♭, F7, and B♭.

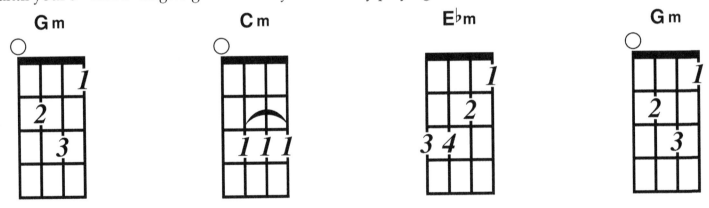

After playing the minor chords above – refer to Exercise No. 3 and borrow the D7 chord for this combination: G mi, C mi, D7, and G mi.

Watch out for a key change on the song "The Streets of Laredo"

The chord combinations in the four keys you've been studying – C, F, G, and B♭ – will enable you to play accompaniments to any number of familiar songs, old and new.

Oh! Susanna

This arrangement copyright by Centerstream Publishing llc

The Streets Of Laredo

This arrangement copyright by Centerstream Publishing llc

36

The Streets Of Laredo

Tiger Rag

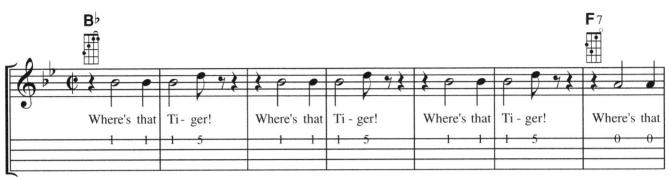

Where's that Ti - ger! Where's that Ti - ger! Where's that Ti - ger! Where's that

Ti - ger! Hold that Ti ger! Hold that Ti - ger! Hold that Ti - ger!

Choke him, poke him, kick him, and soak him! Where's that Ti - ger! Where's that Ti - ger!

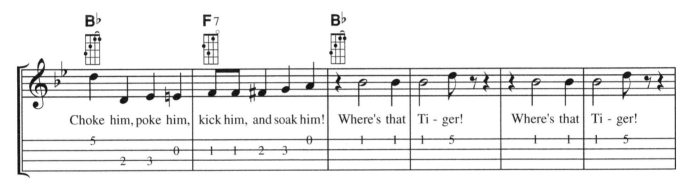

Where, __ oh where __ can he be? __ Low or High - brow,

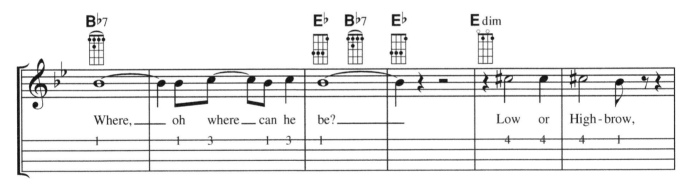

They all cry now: "Please play that Tiger Rag __ for me". That Ti - ger!

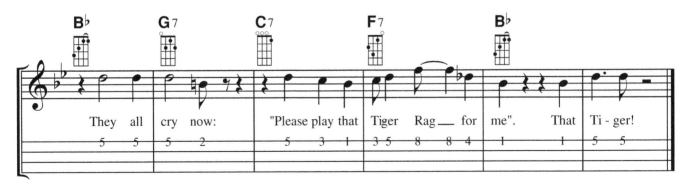

This arrangement copyright by Centerstream Publishing llc

THE DIMINISHED CHORD USED – A "VAMP"

The chord progressions below illustrates a practical use of the diminished chord in a typical chord sequence. These combinations can be used as a "Vamp" or introductions to songs. Learn the progression below and go back to your favorite song and try them out, it sounds great.

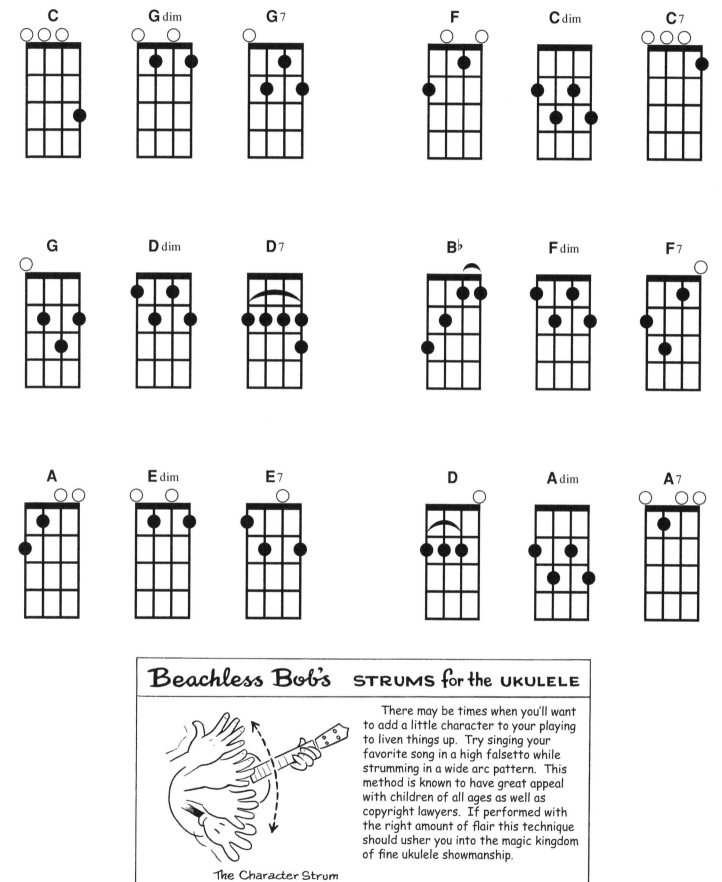

The Character Strum

Beachless Bob's STRUMS for the UKULELE

There may be times when you'll want to add a little character to your playing to liven things up. Try singing your favorite song in a high falsetto while strumming in a wide arc pattern. This method is known to have great appeal with children of all ages as well as copyright lawyers. If performed with the right amount of flair this technique should usher you into the magic kingdom of fine ukulele showmanship.

CROWNED "KING OF THE UKULELE" IN THE 1920s STRING VIRTUOSO BENNIE NAWAHI WAS ONE OF THE FIRST TO PLAY JAZZ ON THE UKE

KING BENNIE NAWAHI

BORN IN HONOLULU IN 1899, BENNIE DEVELOPED AN EARLY LOVE OF MUSIC. SHOWING A NATURAL ABILITY TO PLAY STRING INSTRUMENTS, HE TAUGHT HIMSELF HOW TO PLAY POPULAR TUNES OF THE DAY ON THE SLACK KEY GUITAR AND UKE.

BY THE TIME HE WAS 15 BENNIE WAS PERFORMING FOR SAILORS AND TOURISTS IN HONOLULU'S PARKS MAKING DECENT MONEY IN NICKELS AND DIMES FOR AN EVENING OF PLAYING.

IN 1919 NAWAHI WAS ALSO PERFORMING ON OTHER INSTRUMENTS AND SOON JOINED HIS OLDER BROTHER JOE'S GROUP, THE HAWAIIAN NOVELTY FIVE, PLAYING STEEL GUITAR, MANDOLIN AND UKULELE. THE BAND TOURED THE U.S. MAINLAND ON THE VAUDEVILLE CIRCUIT.

BEFORE LONG BENNIE LEFT THE GROUP TO PURSUE A SOLO CAREER IN VAUDEVILLE AS A SINGER AND UKULELE VIRTUOSO. IT WAS DURING THIS TIME OF THE FIRST UKULELE CRAZE SWEEPING THE U.S. THAT BENNIE EASILY WON PRIZE MONEY OFFERED IN UKULELE CONTESTS HELD IN VARIOUS CITIES BY PLAYING DEMANDING TUNES LIKE "NOLA" and "KITTEN ON THE KEYS".

BENNIE

NAWAHI DAZZLED HIS VAUDEVILLE AUDIENCES WITH HIS UKULELE PYROTECHNICS AND LIVELY STAGE PRESENCE. FOR A SHOW STOPPER HE WOULD PLAY "TURKEY IN THE STRAW" ON THE STEEL GUITAR USING HIS FOOT IN PLACE OF THE STEEL BAR.

BY 1928 HE BEGAN RECORDING WITH A VARIETY OF GROUPS PLAYING NOT ONLY TRADITIONAL HAWAIIAN TUNES, BUT ALSO BLUES, COUNTRY MUSIC and JAZZ. PICKING SINGLE STRING AND CHORD MELODIES HE USED HIS UKE AS AN EFFECTIVE LEAD INSTRUMENT

RECORDING A FEW YEARS LATER WITH JAZZ MUSICIANS IN NEW YORK, BENNIE TRADED HOT SOLOS ON HIS STEEL GUITAR AND UKE WITH OTHERS PLAYING PIANO, SAXOPHONE, VIOLIN PLUS COMB & TISSUE PAPER FOR SOME OF THE BEST SMALL COMBO JAZZ OF THE PERIOD.

IN THE EARLY 1930s BENNIE FORMED HIS OWN GROUP, KING NAWAHI and HIS INTERNATIONAL COWBOYS, TO TOUR THE WEST COAST VAUDEVILLE CIRCUIT. ROY ROGERS, BEFORE HIS RISE TO FAME, WAS ONE OF THE FEATURED VOCALISTS.

BENNIE →

TRAGEDY STRUCK BENNIE IN 1935 WHEN HE SUDDENLY AND INEXPLICABLY WENT BLIND, BUT BLINDNESS DIDN'T KEEP HIM FROM PERFORMING MUSIC. HE CONTINUED TO PLAY AND RECORD WITH HIS NAWAHI TRIO INTO THE 1950's.

NAWAHI WAS ALSO KNOWN FOR HIS PROWESS AS A SWIMMER. IN 1946 HE SWAM THE 26-MILE CHANNEL BETWEEN CATALINA ISLAND AND SAN PEDRO IN 22 HOURS, BATTLING POWERFUL OCEAN CURRENTS WHILE FOLLOWING THE SOUND OF A BELL ATTACHED TO A SMALL BOAT. BENNIE IS STILL THE ONLY BLINDMAN ON RECORD TO ACCOMPLISH THIS FEAT.

NAWAHI CONTINUED PLAYING MUSIC UNTIL THE LATE 1970s WHEN HE SUFFERED A DEBILITATING STROKE

HE DIED IN 1985 AFTER A LONG ILLNESS

©2003 Robt. Armstrong

DID YOU LIKE THIS BOOK? IF SO, CHECK OUT ULTIMATE LIT'L UKULELE CHORDS, PLUS

ULTIMATE LIT'L UKULELE CHORDS, PLUS
by Kahuna Uke (aka Ron Middlebrook)

This handy 6' x 9' guide in the popular C tuning provides all the ukulele chords you'll ever need or use. The diagrams are easy to use and follow, with all the principal chords in major and minor keys, in all the different chords positions. Plus, there are sections on How to Begin, Scales on All Strings, Note Studies, and Chord Modulations (great to use for intros & endings!). This handy 32 page guide fits right in a case perfectly. Happy strumming, you'll Mahalo me latter.

00001351...$7.99

P.O. Box 17878 - Anaheim Hills, CA 92817
(714) 779-9390   www.centerstream-usa.com

More Great Books from Centerstream...

CHRISTMAS UKULELE, HAWAIIAN STYLE

Play your favorite Christmas songs Hawaiian style with expert uke player Chika Nagata. This book/CD pack includes 12 songs, each played 3 times: the first and third time with the melody, the second time without the melody so you can play or sing along with the rhythm-only track. Songs include: Mele Kalikimaka (Merry Christmas to You) • We Wish You a Merry Christmas • Jingle Bells (with Hawaiian lyrics) • Angels We Have Heard on High • Away in a Manger • Deck the Halls • Hark! The Herald Angels Sing • Joy to the World • O Come, All Ye Faithful • Silent Night • Up on the Housetop • We Three Kings.
00000472 Book/CD Pack $19.95

FUN SONGS FOR UKULELE

50 terrific songs in standard notation and tablature for beginning to advanced ukulele players. Includes Hawaiian songs, popular standards, classic Western, Stephen Foster and more, with songs such as: The Darktown Strutters Ball • I'm Always Chasing Rainbows • Hot Lips • Gentle Annie • Maikai Waipio • Whispering • Ja-Da • China Boy • Colorado Trail • and many more. Also includes a chord chart and a special section on how to hold the ukulele.
00000407..$14.95

THE HAWAIIAN STEEL GUITAR AND ITS GREAT HAWAIIAN MUSICIANS

compiled & edited by Lorene Ruymar
This fascinating book takes a look at Hawaiian music; the origin of the steel guitar and how it spread throughout the world; Hawaiian playing styles, techniques and tunings; and more.
00000192 208 pages $34.95

UKULELE FOR COWBOYS

40 of your favorite cowboy songs in chords, standard notation and tab. Includes: Buffalo Gals • Night Herding Song • Doney Gal • Old Chisholm Trail • The Big Corral • Ragtime Cowboy Joe • Colorado Trail • Old Paint • Yellow Rose of Texas • Green Grow the Lilacs • and many more. Also includes a chord chart, historical background on many of the songs, and a short story on the history of the Hawaiian Cowboy.
00000408...$14.99

UKULELE SONGBOOK

compiled by Ron Middlebrook
This terrific collection for beginning to advanced ukulele players features easy arrangements of 50 great songs, in standard notation and tablature. Also teaches popular strum patterns, and how to tune the uke.
00000248...$9.95

UKULELE CHORDS
Plus Intros and Endings

by Ron Middlebrook
This handy chart includes clear, easy-to-see chord fingerings in all keys, plus a bonus section that provides favorite intros and endings in different keys. Also includes information on relative tuning.
00000246...$2.95

New! *Ukulele Pitch Pipe in C Tuning,* **$6.99**

New! *Ukulele Strings, In Black or Clear Nylon,* **$6.99** *per set.*

New! *Ukulele Strap, "Take the pressure off your fretting hand".* **$8.99**

P.O. Box 17878 - Anaheim Hills, CA 92817
(714) 779-9390   www.centerstream-usa.com

Those using Centerstream Books & DVDs

The Competition